# Amazing Lizards

Written by Carol Krueger

## CONTENTS

# Amazing Lizards

Lizards are reptiles. Some are big and some are small.

Some lizards can do amazing things. They can walk across water. They can walk upside down. They can see in different directions at the same time. They can fly through the air. They can lose their tails and grow new ones. They can even change their colour and size.

This lizard is small.

This lizard is big.

# How Lizards Move in Amazing Ways

Some lizards can move their eyes in an amazing way.

These lizards have two very large eyes. They can look in two different directions at the same time. When they hunt, they use one eye to look for an insect to eat. They use the other eye to watch out for enemies.

chameleon

chameleon

Some lizards catch food with their tongues.

This lizard's tongue is longer than its body. It is covered with sticky spit.

When the lizard sees an insect, it puts out its tongue. The tongue can move very quickly. The insect gets stuck on the tongue. Then the lizard pulls in the insect.

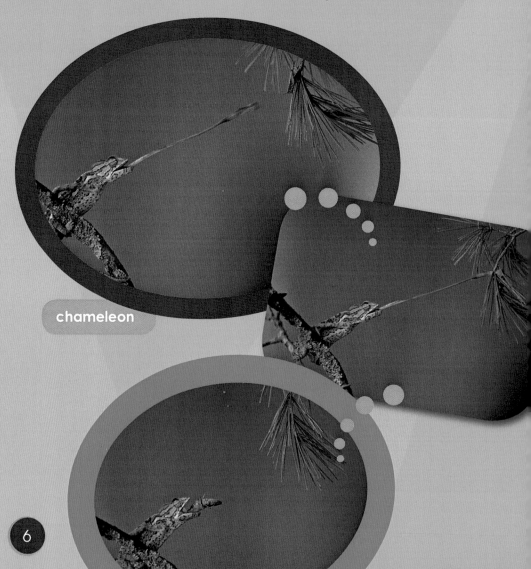

chameleon

Some lizards can walk on water. Their back legs are shaped like a frog's legs.

When this lizard is scared, it runs across the water on its back legs. It uses its tail for balance. It runs very fast, so it doesn't sink into the water.

This lizard can run 400 metres on water!

This lizard can walk upside down along the ceiling without falling off.

It has flat, round toes. The toes uncurl as it walks.

On the toes are lots of tiny hairs. The hairs help the lizard to hold on. They can grip so well, the lizard can hang from the ceiling by one toe!

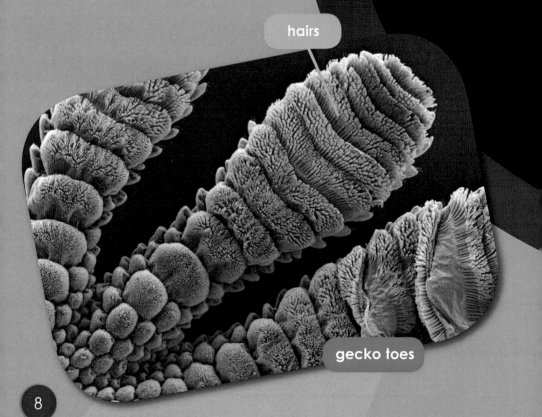

hairs

gecko toes

geckos

# How Lizards Change in Amazing Ways

These lizards can change their colour.

When they are angry, they can turn black. If they are frightened, they can turn pale. If they are sleepy, they can turn tan. And, if they are calm, they can turn green.

When they fight, they turn bright colours. But, if they lose the fight, they might turn yellow.

Chameleons can go from one colour to another in 15 seconds!

Some lizards can change their size.

This lizard can change the size of its body.
When it is frightened, it lifts up its skin collar.
This makes the lizard look much bigger
than it is.

The skin collar is held up by long bones.
When the enemy has gone, the lizard folds
the collar back around its neck.

frilled lizard

This lizard's collar has
another use. It can store
insects in the folds.

Some lizards can take a really deep breath, and puff up their whole body so they become bigger. They do this to scare other lizards.

bearded dragon lizard

This lizard has scales on its throat that are long and pointed. They look like a beard. If the lizard sees an enemy, it hisses and pushes out its beard. Then the lizard looks bigger.

13

# How Some Lizards Escape

Some lizards escape from danger by flying through the air.

This lizard can glide between trees to escape from enemies.

It has large flaps of skin on each side of its body. These flaps are like wings. When it wants to fly, it opens the flaps. As the lizard glides through the air, it uses the wings like a parachute.

When it lands, it closes the skin flaps.

A flying dragon lizard can glide for 20 metres!

14

Some lizards escape from an enemy by losing their tail.

This lizard can lose its tail. When the tail falls off, it keeps moving. While the enemy is watching this, the lizard escapes.

A new tail will grow back, but it can be a different colour and have no bones.

Sometimes a lizard's tail does not break right off. The tail will heal while another one grows. Then the lizard will have two tails!

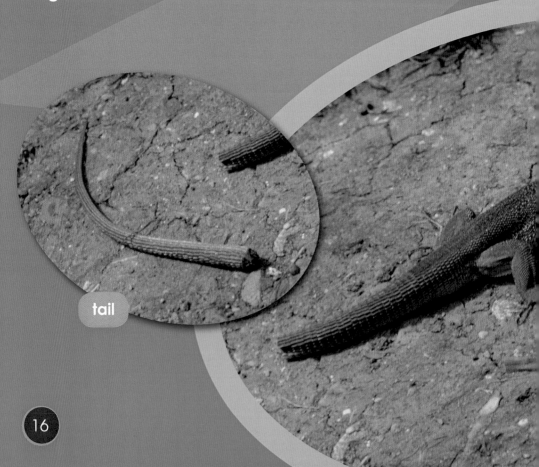

tail

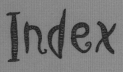

# Index

# Explanations

Amazing Lizards is an **Explanation**.

An explanation explains **how** or **why** things happen.

An explanation has a topic:

## Amazing Lizards

An explanation has headings:

## How Lizards Move in Amazing Ways

## How Lizards Change in Amazing Ways

## How Some Lizards Escape

## Some information is put under headings.

### How Lizards Move in Amazing Ways

**A chameleon's eyes move separately.**

**It can look in two directions at once.**

## Information can be shown in other ways.
## This explanation has . . .

Labels   Captions   Photographs

frilled lizard

This lizard's collar has another use. It can store insects in the folds.

# ▬▬ Guide Notes

**Title: Amazing Lizards**
**Stage:** Fluency

**Text Form:** Informational Explanation
**Approach:** Guided Reading
**Processes:** Thinking Critically, Exploring Language, Processing Information
**Written and Visual Focus:** Contents Page, Labels, Captions, Index

## THINKING CRITICALLY
(sample questions)

### Before Reading – Establishing Prior Knowledge
• What do you know about lizards?

### Visualising the Text Content
• What might you expect to see in this book?
• What form of writing do you think will be used by the author?
Look at the contents page and index. Encourage the students to think about the information and make predictions about the text content.

### After Reading – Interpreting the Text
• Why do you think it is important for a lizard to keep an eye out for enemies?
• What features do you think could help the basilisk lizard walk on water?
  Why do you think this?
• How do you think being able to walk upside down on the ceiling could help the gecko?
• Why might a chameleon turn a bright colour when it is fighting?
• Do you think the frilled lizard is brave? Why do you think this?
• Do you think losing a tail is a good way for a lizard to keep safe from danger?
  Why do you think this?
• What do you know about lizards that you didn't know before?
• What in the book helped you understand the information?
• What questions do you have after reading the text?

## EXPLORING LANGUAGE

### Terminology
Photography credits, index, contents page, imprint information, ISBN number